# NON- PROFIT ACCOUNTING AND BOOKKEEPING

## ACCOUNTING FOR CLUBS, SOCIETIES AND CHURCHES

Toye Adelaja

# TABLE OF CONTENTS

Chapter 1

## NON-PROFIT- ORIENTED ORGANIZATION

1.1.    Non-Profit-oriented Organizations

Charities, clubs, societies, associations and other non-profit oriented organizations do not prepare income statements because their objectives are not to make profits. Their members only come together to undertake things in common. They do things such as playing football, table tennis, golf, and do other legal things together.

Non-profit-oriented organizations can also be referred to as non-trading organizations. They include churches, Mosques, Clubs, Societies and other charitable organizations. They derive their income from any or combinations of the following:
a.  Subscription
b.  Membership fee
c.  Fines
d.  Subventions
e.  Investment income
f.  Donations from public or government
g.  Profit from operating bars and restaurants
h.  Grants from government
i.  Statutory allocation
j.  Organizing lecture and symposia
k.  Tithe
l.  Offering
m.  Special offering


Rather than preparing income statements, they prepare income and expenditure accounts, and receipts and payments accounts. There are many **differences between receipts and payments accounts and income and expenditure accounts**.

**1.2. Receipts and Payments accounts**

Receipts and payments accounts are a summary of the cash transactions that take place in a particular accounting period. Profit oriented organizations prepare cash book to capture all cash transactions of their business but non- profit organizations prepares receipt and payments instead.

## 1.3. Income and Expenditure Accounts

Where assets are owned by a non-profit oriented organization and liabilities are owed by it, receipts and payments alone are not enough to display information about such organization. Hence, the following are required:

1. A statement of financial position
2. Income and expenditure accounts

A statement of financial position shows what the organization own and what is owed to the organization while income and expenditure shows the amount by which **accumulated fund** (capital) has been increased or decreased.

1.4. Differences Between Non-profit Oriented Organizations and Profit Oriented Organizations.

The following are the terminologies distinguishing non-profit - oriented organization from profit- oriented organization:

| Profit-oriented organization | Non-profit-oriented organization |
|---|---|
| 1. Income Statement | Income and expenditure Account |
| 2. Net profit | Surplus of income over expenditure |
| 3.Net loss | Deficit of income over expenditure |
| 4. Capital | Accumulated fund |
| 5. Cash book | Receipts and Payments |

Differences between Receipts and Payments accounts and Income and Expenditure accounts are as follows:

1. Receipts and payments account usually has opening balance of cash or bank balance or overdraft while income and expenditure does not have opening balance.
2. Depreciation of non-current asset is not recorded on receipt and payment accounts while depreciation is recorded on income and expenditure accounts.
3. Receipt and payment accounts are recorded on **cash basis** while income and expenditure accounts are recorded on **accrual basis**.
4. Receipt and payment accounts represent a cash book summary while income and expenditure accounts represent statement of comprehensive income of a commercial business.
5. Capital items are recorded on receipt and payment accounts while capital items are totally excluded from income and expenditure accounts.

6. Income and revenue are recorded on the debit side of receipt and payment account while expenditure are recorded on the debit side of income and expenditure accounts

Cash Basis

Cash basis is an accounting process that states that accounting transaction should be recorded only when cash is exchange. It states that revenue is recognized at the time cash is collected and expenditure should be recorded only when cash is spent on it.

## 1.3.1 ACCUMULATED FUND

Accumulated fund represents the capital of non-profit oriented organization. A sole trader has capital account while a non-profit-oriented organization has accumulated fund.

For a sole proprietor:

Capital $=$ Assets $-$ Liabilities

For a non-profit-oriented organization:

Accumulated fund = Assets – Liabilities

In some cases, accumulated fund may not be provided in the examination questions. You may need to determine the accumulated fund. All you need to do is to prepare a statement of affairs as at the start of the period to determine the accumulated fund.

The items to be considered in the ascertainment of accumulated fund would include assets and liabilities for the previous year. The difference between the two produces closing balance of accumulated fund for the previous year and opening balance for the current year.

ILLUSTRATION 1

The following were extracted from the books of M.K club as at 31$^{st}$ December, 2014:

|                      | $       |
|----------------------|---------|
| Furniture            | 400,000 |
| Sport kit            | 700,000 |
| Club house           | 650,000 |
| Subscription prepaid | 10,000  |
| Bar Creditors        | 312,000 |
| Subscription owing   | 80,000  |

You are required to compute the accumulated fund as at the period ended.

SOLUTION

Statements of affairs as at 31st December,2014

|  | $ | $ |
|---|---|---|
| Assets |  |  |
| Furniture |  | 400,000 |
| Sport Kit |  | 700,000 |
| Club house |  | 650,000 |
| Subscription owing |  | 80,000 |
|  |  | 1,830,000 |
| Less: |  |  |
| Bar Creditors | 312,000 |  |
| Subscription prepaid | 10,000 |  |
|  | 322,000 | -322,000 |
| Accumulated fund |  | 1,508,000 |

₦1,508,000 is the opening balance of accumulated fund as at 1st January, 2015.

Note: **Subscription owing** by a member is a current asset to the organization while **subscription prepaid** is a liability to the organization. Subscription owed by members or paid by members are recorded on subscription accounts

## 1.3.2. SUBSCRIPTION

The preparation of subscription account could pose problems for students. .The format below would be of help.

### Subscription Accounts

|  | $ |  | $ |
|---|---|---|---|
| Owing from the previous year b/f | xx | Prepaid from the previous year b/f | xx |
| Income and expenditure A/C | | Total received during the year | xx |
| (difference) | xx | Bad debts(if any) | xx |

| prepaid for the next year c/d | xx | owing at the end of the year | xx |
| | xx | | xx |

This above format can also be used to prepare subventions accounts and other income accounts. It is only the title that changes but the format remains the same.

ILLUSTRATION 1

The following information relates to a Tennis club:

|  | $ |
|---|---|
| Subscription owing at the beginning | 160 |
| Subscription owing at the end | 130 |
| Subscription received in advance at the Beginning | 50 |
| Subscription received during the accounting period | 5,120 |

You are required to prepare subscription for the year.

SOLUTION 1

### Subscription

Accounts

| | $ | | $ |
|---|---|---|---|
| Owing b/d | 160 | Prepaid b/d | 50 |
| Income and expenditure | 5,140 | Cash | 5120 |
| for the year | | Owing c/d | 130 |
| | 5,300 | | 5,300 |

ILLUSTRATION 2

A football club charges its members an annual subscription of $500 per member. It accrues for subscription owing at the end of each year and also adjusts for subscription received in advance.

A) On 1 January 2012, 9 members had not yet paid their subscriptions for the year 2011.
B) In December 2011, 2 members paid $1,000 for the year 2012.
C) During the year 2012 it received $185,500 in cash for

subscriptions

|  | $ |
|---|---|
| For 2011 | 9,000 |
| For 2012 | 173,000 |
| For 2013 | 3,500 |

D) At 31 December 2012, 5 members had not paid their 2012 subscription.

You are required to compute the subscription that will be recorded in income and expenditure accounts for the year 2012.

SOLUTION 2

Subscription for the year 2012

| | $ | | $ |
|---|---|---|---|
| Owing b/f | 4500 | Prepaid b/f | 1,000 |
| Income | | | |
| (P&L) | 181,000 | Cash | 185,500 |
| Prepaid c/d | 3500 | Owing c/d | 2,500 |
| | 189,000 | | 189,000 |

# Chapter 2

## Accounting for Non-Trading Organizations and Profit or Loss for a special purposes

Occasionally, there are special situations that necessitate a non-profit –oriented organization to prepare a trading account or an income statement.

### 2.1. Clubs and Societies

For example a table tennis club may organize a dancing competition inviting people to come and watch and pay entrance fee. The money generated from this dance competition can be used to pay table tennis expenses. For this dance competition, a trading or a full income statement could be drawn up. The profit or loss reported will be transferred to income and expenditure accounts.

Another example is when a club operates a bar or restaurant. It is necessary to prepare bar trading accounts: Example of likely information are:
1. Payment for Bar supplies in the receipt and payment or Bank Account.
2. Bar Takings
3. Bar man wages
4. Inventory of refreshment (opening and closing)
   It may be necessary to determine Bar purchases for a particular period.. **Purchases ledger control** account can be used to determine the Bar purchases. **Sales Ledger control accounts** can be used to determine bar sales where it is required.

### 2.2.1 Life Membership

It is allowed in some clubs and societies for members to make a payment for life membership. This means by paying a fairly large amount for subscription, members will be able to enjoy the facilities of the club for the rest of their lives.

Such receipt should not be treated in the income and expenditure account solely in the year in which the money was received from the members. The whole amount paid by the members should be recorded in the life membership account and appropriate amount should be transferred from it to the income and expenditure account annually.

What is the appropriate amount to be transferred to income and expenditure annually?

This can be determined by the ages of members that normally join the club. For example, A golf club is known for youth. A great number of members of the club will be composed of youth. As a result of this many years are required for the life membership due/subscription to get exhausted, and hence great number of years should be used to average the amount paid by the members.

2.2.2.  Donation

The full amount of donation received should be recorded in the income and expenditure account in the year it is collected.

2.2.3. Entrance Fees

When members initially join a club, in addition to the membership fee for that year, new members often have to pay an entrance fee. Entrance fees are normally included as income in the year in which it was collected and posted to income and expenditure immediately.

# ILLUSTRATION 1

The following are extracted from the books of Vilili Rotary Club.

Receipt and payment as the year ended 31st December, 2009.

| | $ | | $ |
|---|---|---|---|
| Balance b/d | 2,000 | Salaries | 4,000 |
| Subscription | 30,000 | Rent | 2,000 |
| | | Rates | 3,000 |
| | | Electricity expenses | 1,000 |
| | | Balance c/d | 22,000 |
| | 32,000 | | 32,000 |
| Balance b/d | 22,000 | | |

| | 1st January, 2009 | 31st December, 2009 |
|---|---|---|
| | $ | $ |
| Equipment | 120,000 | 120,000 |
| Rent(accrued) | 400 | 500 |
| Rates(prepaid) | 600 | 800 |
| Subscription in arrears | 3,000 | 2,000 |
| Subscription in advance | 2,600 | 1600 |

You are required to calculate:

a.  the accumulated fund as at 1st January, 2009

b.  the amount of subscription that will appear on the credit side of income and expenditure account for the year 2009?

SOLUTION

(a)

Statement of affairs as at 1st Jan. 2009

|  | $ | $ |
|---|---|---|
| Equipment |  | 120,000 |
| Rent |  | 600 |
| Subscription in arrears |  | 3000 |
| Cash |  | 2,000 |
|  |  | 125,600 |
| Less: |  |  |
| Rent (accrual) | 400 |  |
| Subscription in advance | 2,600 | -3,000 |
| Accumulated fund |  | 122,600 |

(b)

Subscription Accounts for the year ended 31st Dec. 2009

|  | $ |  | $ |
|---|---|---|---|
| In arrears b/d | 3,000 | In advance b/d | 2,600 |
| In advance c/d | 1,600 | Bank | 30,000 |
| Income& Expenditure | 30,000 | In arrears | 2,000 |
|  | 34,600 |  | 34,600 |

the amount of subscription that will appear on the credit side of income and expenditure account for the year 2009 is $30,000.

ILLUSTRATION 2

Income and Expenditure Account

|  | $ |  | $ |
|---|---|---|---|
| Wages | 28,000 | Subscription received | 60,000 |
| Electricity | 10,000 | Donations | 30,000 |
| Depreciation of furniture | 3000 | Profit on sales of cars | 5,000 |
| Other expenses | ? |  |  |

| Excess of income over expenditure | ? | | | |
|---|---|---|---|---|
| | 95,000 | | | 95,000 |

It is the tradition of the club to write off an amount equal to 30% of the subscription received as other expenses.

a) What is the amount to be written off other expenses?

b) What is the amount of the surplus?

SOLUTION TO ILLUSTRATION 2

a)
$30\% \times 60,000 = \$18,000$

b)
$\$95,000 - \$28,000 - \$10,000 - \$3,000 = \$36,000$

ILLUSTRATION 3

On the trial balance of pop up social club, the following debit and credit balances were listed as at 31st December, 1998.

| | $ | $ |
|---|---|---|
| Accumulated Fund | | 11,700 |
| Secretary salary | 240 | |
| Subscription | | 980 |
| Proceeds from dance | | 290 |
| Proceeds from raffle | | 200 |
| Expenses on dance | 56 | |
| Printing of raffle tickets | 150 | |
| Postage | 50 | |
| Clubhouse | 11,800 | |
| Insurance | 48 | |
| Furniture and fittings | 300 | |

| | $ | | | $ |
|---|---|---|---|---|
| cash at bank | 470 | | | |
| Cash in hand | 16 | | | |
| Subscription (1997) in arrears | 40 | | | |
| | 13,170 | 13,170 | | |

Prepare the income and expenditure account of the club for the year ended 31st December, 1998 and the balance sheet as that date, taking the following adjustments into consideration:

i. of the subscription figure $40 is in respect of 1997 arrears and $56 has been paid in advance for 1999.

ii. the clubhouse is to be depreciated at the rate of 1% per annum while furniture and fittings are to be depreciated at the rate of 10% per annum.

iii. out of insurance figure, $16 has been paid in advance.

iv. the secretary is on a salary of $300 per annum and the balance of unpaid salary is to be provided for.

## SOLUTION TO ILLUSTARTION 3

Income and Expenditure Account for the period ended 31st Dec. 1998

| | $ | | $ |
|---|---|---|---|
| Secretary salary | 300 | Subscription | 884 |
| postage | 50 | Profit from dance | 234 |
| Insurance | 32 | Profit from raffle | 50 |
| Depreciation: | | | |
| clubhouse | 118 | | |
| Furniture & Fittings | 30 | | |
| Excess of | | | |

| income over expenditure | 638 | | | |
|---|---|---|---|---|
| | 1168 | | 1168 | |

## Statement of financial position as at 31st December, 1998.

| Non Current Assets | $ | $ | $ |
|---|---|---|---|
| Clubhouse | | 11,800 | |
| Less Depreciation | | -118 | |
| | | | 11,682 |
| Furniture & Fittings | | 300 | |
| Less Depreciation | | -30 | 270 |
| | | | 11,952 |
| Current Assets | | | |
| Prepaid insurance | | 16 | |
| Bank balance | | 470 | |
| Cash balance | | 16 | |
| | | 502 | |
| Current Liabilities | | | |
| Subscriptionin advance | 56 | | |
| Secretary salary | 60 | | |
| | | -116 | |
| Working capital | | | 386 |
| Net Assets | | | 12,338 |
| Accumulated fund | | | 11,700 |
| Add: Excess of income over Expenditure | | | 638 |
| | | | 12,338 |

Workings
1) Subscription Accounts

| | $ | | $ |
|---|---|---|---|
| Owing b/f | 40 | cash | 980 |
| income & | | | |
| Exp. | 884 | | |
| Advance c/d | 56 | | |
| | 980 | | 980 |

3) Profit from raffles:           $
    Proceeds                      200
    Less:Expenditure on tickets   150
                                   50

4) Profit from Dance              $
    Proceeds from dance           290
    Less: Expenses on dance       56
                                  234

## 2.2. Accounting for Churches

Churches are parts of the organizations established not for the purpose of profit making. However, the records of all activities of churches must be kept properly.

Accounting for churches follows the same procedures for societies and all other non- profit oriented organization. The few differences between accounting for churches and other non-trading organization are the terms that are peculiar to churches.

For instance, the following incomes are peculiar to churches:

1) Tithe
2) Offering
3) Special offering
4) Donations

5) Funds raising
6) Special offering call
7) Thanksgiving offering

Chapter 3

Quiz

Understanding and Mastering of Non- profit oriented organization can also be better explained by practicing in quiz or multi-choice questions and answers. As a result of this, a series of multi-choice questions and answers are included here.

1. In a not-for-profit organization, the excess of income over expenditure is
   A.  added to cash balance.
   B.  added to capital
   C.  deducted from accumulated fund.
   D.  added to accumulated fund.

2. The equivalent of club's statement of comprehensive income is
   A. Revenue Accounts
   B. Profit and Loss Accounts
   C. Income and Expenditure Accounts
   D. Receipts and Payment Accounts

3. The difference between assets and liabilities of a club or society is
   A. Capital  B. Equity  C. Accumulated fund  D. Working capital

4. Subscription in advance is treated in the balance sheet of a club as
   A. Current asset
   B. Current liability
   C. Reserve
   D. Fictitious asset

5. Which of the following is a credit item on an income and expenditure accounts?
   A. Salaries
   B. Bar expenses
   C. Subscription
   D. Rates

6. The equivalent of a club's Receipt and Payment accounts is a
A. Trading account
B. Cash Book
C. Profit and Loss Account
D. Revenue accounts

7. A non-profit-making organization differs from a profit making one in that
   A. it does not earn income
   B. proceeds from sale of shares form part of its income
   C. all its income is committed
   D. annual subscriptions and levies form part of its income

8. Subscription in advance is an example of ……….in the book of a club.
   A. accrual
   B. deposit
   C. prepayment
   D. receivables

9. Income and expenditure accounts is based on
   A. Accrual Accounting
   B. Cash accounting
   C. Financial Accounting
   D. Management Accounting

10. The debit balance on the receipt and payment account of a non-profit organization
     is regarded as a

   A. Current liability
   B. Current Asset
   C. Accrual
   D. Prepayment

11. Which of the following is the accounting equation for non-profit organization?
A. Asset = Capital + Liability

B. Asset = Liability + Fund
C. Accumulated fund + Liability = Asset
D. Capital = Asset − liability

12. A non-profit organization received $6,000 as the entrance fee of a new member. If 15% of the fee has to be capitalized, what is the amount of fee needed to be shown in the income and expenditure account?
A. $6,100
B. B. $900
C. C.$ 5,100
D. D.$ 7,500

13. The end result of Income and expenditure accounts of a club shows
A. Net Profit or Net Loss
B. Gross Profit
C. Surplus or deficit
E. Cash available to the club

14. When cash is received for life membership, which of the following double entries is recorded?
    A. Debit life membership account and credit income and expenditure account
    B. Debit life membership accounts and credit cash accounts
    C. Debit cash accounts and credit life membership accounts
    D. Debit life membership accounts and credit investment

15. Depreciation of an asset is matched against the revenue of a not-for profit organization in its
A. cash book
B.profit and loss account
C.income and expenditure account
D. accumulated depreciation

16. When cash is received for life membership, which of the following double entries is recorded?

A. Debit life membership account and credit income and expenditure account
B. Debit life membership accounts and credit cash accounts
C. Debit cash accounts and credit life membership accounts
D. Debit life membership accounts and credit investment

17. Depreciation of an asset is matched against the revenue of a not-for profit organization in its
   A. cash book
   B.profit and loss account
   C.income and expenditure account
   D. accumulated depreciation

18. Which of the following is not an item of receipt and payment accounts?
   A. Donation
   B. Depreciation
   C. honourarium
   D. subscription

19. Subscription received but not yet earned is recorded under
A. assets
B. current liabilities
C. equity
D. non- current assets

20. Which of the following will not be found in the statement of financial position of a non-profit-oriented organization?
A. assets
B. liabilities
C. accumulated funds
D. owners' equity

21. Investment in sinking fund by a non-profit-oriented organization is know as
A. assets
B. liabilities
C. bonds

D. expenditures

22. Which of the following are sources of income for non-trading organization?
    i. donation   ii. government subvention   iii. subscription  iv. Proceeds from social
    activities   v. proceed from disposal of asset   vi. government bond
    A. i,ii,iii and iv only  B. ii and vi only
    C. i, ii, iii, iv and v only   D. i, ii, iii, iv, v and vi only

23. A statement of affairs as at the start of an accounting period is drawn up to determine which of the following?
    A. Share of profit due to members
    B. subscription owed
    C. capital
    D. accumulated fund

24. In a non-profit-oriented organization, depreciation of asset is recorded to which account?
    A. profit and loss accounts
    B. receipt and payment accounts
    C. trading accounts
    D. income and expenditure accounts

25. On what basis is the receipt and payment accounts prepared?
    A. accrual basis
    B. commitment basis
    C. cash basis
    D. income basis

26. The main purpose of preparing income and expenditure accounts is to determine
A. Net profit or loss for the period
B. Gross profit or loss for the period
C. Accumulated fund for the period
D. Surplus or deficit for the period

27. Which of the following is the accounting basis for recording donation received by a non-profit-oriented organization?

A. cash basis
B. accrual basis
C. materiality
D. commitment basis

28. An amount paid as honorarium by non-profit-oriented organization is
A. debited to statement of comprehensive income
B. credited to income and expenditure accounts
C. debited to income and expenditure accounts
D. transferred to members of the organization

## SOLUTION TO MULTI CHOICE QUESTIONS

| | | |
|---|---|---|
| 1. D | 11. C | 21. A |
| 2. C | 12. C | 22. C |
| 3. C | 13. C | 23. D |
| 4. B | 14. C | 24. D |
| 5. C | 15. C | 25. C |
| 6. B | 16. C | 26. D |
| 7. D | 17. C | 27. A |
| 8. A | 18. B | 28. C |
| 9. A | 19. B | |
| 10. B | 20. D | |

Workings

12. $6,000×85% = $5,100

# REFERENCES

Toye Adelaja(2015) Basic Financial Accounting(MCQ & A)

www.ingramcontent.com/pod-product-compliance
Lightning Source LLC
Chambersburg PA
CBHW070928180526
45168CB00005B/2195